This book belongs to

....

First published in 2021 by Miles Kelly Publishing Ltd
Harding's Barn, Bardfield End Green, Thaxted, Essex, CM6 3PX, UK

2 4 6 8 10 9 7 5 3

Publishing Director Belinda Gallagher
Creative Director Jo Cowan
Editorial Director Rosie Neave
Senior Editor Fran Bromage
Cover Designer Jo Cowan
Design Manager Joe Jones
Image Manager Liberty Newton
Production Elizabeth Collins
Reprographics Stephan Davis
Assets Venita Kidwai

ISBN 978-1-78989-895-8

Printed in China

British Library Cataloging-in-Publication Data
A catalog record for this book is available from the British Library

ACKNOWLEDGMENTS
The publishers would like to thank the following artists who have contributed to this book:
Advocate Art: Angela Muss, Helen Poole, Pope Twins,
Sophia Touliatou (inc. cover), Hannah Wood
The Bright Agency: Barbara Bakos, Sharon Harmer
Luciana Feito
All other artwork from the Miles Kelly Artwork Bank

Made with paper from a sustainable forest

www.mileskelly.net

100 Nursery Rhymes

Contents

OLD MacDONALD had a Farm

Old Macdonald had
a farm, E-I-E-I-O!
And on that farm he had some
cows, E-I-E-I-O!
With a moo-moo here,
And a moo-moo there,
Here a moo, there a moo,
Everywhere a moo-moo,
Old Macdonald had a farm,
E-I-E-I-O!

Old Macdonald had a farm, E-I-E-I-O!
And on that farm he had some
sheep, E-I-E-I-O!
With a baa-baa here,
And a baa-baa there,
Here a baa, there a baa,
Everywhere a baa-baa,
Old Macdonald had a farm, E-I-E-I-O!

Old Macdonald had a farm, E-I-E-I-O!
And on that farm he had some
ducks, E-I-E-I-O!
With a quack-quack here,
And a quack-quack there,
Here a quack, there a quack,
Everywhere a quack-quack,
Old Macdonald had a farm,
E-I-E-I-O!

Old Macdonald had a farm, E-I-E-I-O!
And on that farm he had some
pigs, E-I-E-I-O!
With an oink-oink here,
And an oink-oink there,
Here an oink, there an oink,
Everywhere an oink-oink,
Old Macdonald had a farm, E-I-E-I-O!

Hickory, Dickory, Dock

Hickory, dickory, dock!
The mouse ran up the clock.
The clock struck one,
The mouse ran down,
Hickory, dickory, dock!

Three Blind Mice

Three blind mice,
three blind mice,
See how they run,
see how they run!
They all ran after the
farmer's wife,
Who cut off their tails
with a carving knife,
Did you ever see such a
thing in your life,
As three blind mice?

Pat-a-cake

Pat-a-cake, pat-a-cake, baker's man,
Bake me a cake as fast as you can.
Pat it and prick it, and
mark it with "B,"
And put it in the oven
For Baby and me.

I'm
a Little
Teapot

I'm a little teapot
Short and stout,
Here is my handle
Here is my spout.

When I see the teacups
Hear me shout,
"Tip me up and pour me out!"

15

The Turtle

There was a little turtle
Who lived in a box.

He swam
in the puddles
And climbed on the rocks.

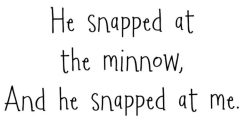

He snapped at
the minnow,
And he snapped at me.

He snapped at
the mosquito,
He snapped at the flea.

He caught the
mosquito,
He caught the flea.

He caught the minnow,
But he didn't catch me!

Wee Willie Winkie

Wee Willie Winkie
Runs through the town,
Upstairs and downstairs
In his nightgown.
Rapping at the window,
Crying through the lock,
"Are the children in their beds,
For now it's eight o'clock?"

19

Sing a Song of Sixpence

Sing a song of sixpence,
A pocket full of rye.
Four and twenty blackbirds,
Baked in a pie.

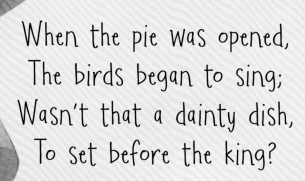

When the pie was opened,
The birds began to sing;
Wasn't that a dainty dish,
To set before the king?

The king was in his
counting house,
Counting out his money;
The queen was
in the parlor,
Eating bread and honey.

The maid was in the garden,
Hanging out the clothes;
When down came a blackbird
And pecked off her nose!

High in the Pine Tree

High in the pine tree,
The little turtledove
Made a little nursery
To please her little love.

"Coo," said the turtledove,
"Coo," said she,
In the long
shady branches
Of the dark pine tree.

The Hobbyhorse

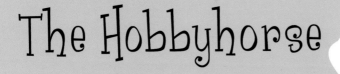

I had a little hobbyhorse,
And it was dapple gray;
Its head was made of pea-straw,
Its tail was made of hay.

I sold it to an old woman
For a copper groat;
And I'll not sing my song again
Without another coat.

One, Two, Buckle my Shoe

One, two,
buckle my shoe.

Three, four,
knock at the door.

24

Five, six, pick up sticks.

Seven, eight, lay them straight.

Nine, ten,
a good fat hen.

Oh Dear, what can the Matter be?

Oh dear, what can the matter be?
Dear, dear, what can the matter be?
Oh dear, what can the matter be?
Johnny's so long at the fair.

He promised to bring me
a basket of posies,
A garland of lilies,
a garland of roses,
A little straw hat,
to set off the ribbons
That tie up my bonny brown hair.

Head, Shoulders, Knees, and Toes

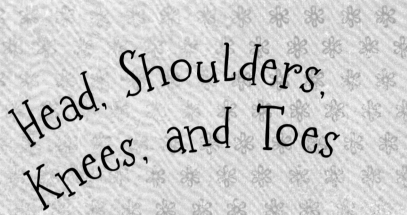

Head, shoulders, knees,
and toes,
Knees and toes.

28

Head, shoulders, knees, and toes,
Knees and toes.
And eyes and ears and mouth and nose,
Head, shoulders, knees, and toes,
Knees and toes.

Little Tommy Tittlemouse

Little Tommy Tittlemouse
Lived in a little house;
He caught fishes
In other mens' ditches.

Ride a Toy Horse

Ride a toy horse to Banbury Cross,
To see a fine lady upon a white horse;
Rings on her fingers and bells on her toes,
And she shall have music wherever she goes.

31

A Candle, a Candle

A candle, a candle to light me to bed,
A pillow, a pillow to tuck up my head.
The moon is as sleepy as sleepy can be,
The stars are all pointing
their fingers at me.

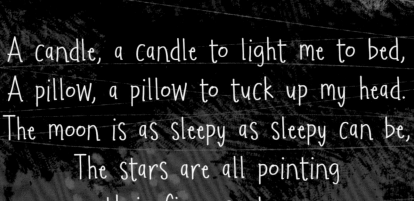

And Missus Hop-robin, way up in her nest,
Is rocking her tired little babies to rest.
So give me a blanket to tuck up my toes,
And a little soft pillow to snuggle my nose.

Monday's Child

Monday's child is
fair of face,

Tuesday's child is
full of grace,

Wednesday's child
is full of woe,

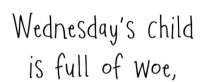

Thursday's child
has far to go,

34

Friday's child is
loving and giving,

Saturday's child works
hard for a living,

But the child that
is born on the
Sabbath day,
Is bonny and blithe
and good and gay.

I See the Moon

I see the moon,
And the moon sees me.
God bless the moon,
And God bless me!

Five Little Peas

Five little peas
In a peapod pressed,
One grew, two grew,
And so did all the rest.
They grew and grew
And did not stop,
Until one day
The peapod popped!

A Cat came Fiddling

A cat came fiddling out of a barn,
With a pair of bagpipes under her arm.
She could sing nothing but fiddle dee dee,
The mouse has married the bumblebee.
Pipe, cat; dance, mouse;
We'll have a wedding at our good house.

39

If You're Happy and You Know it

If you're happy and you know it,
Clap your hands!
If you're happy and you know it,
Clap your hands!
If you're happy and you know it
And you really want to show it,
If you're happy and you know it
Clap your hands!

HUMPTY DUMPTY

Humpty Dumpty sat on a wall,
Humpty Dumpty had
a great fall
All the king's horses and
all the king's men
Couldn't put Humpty
together again.

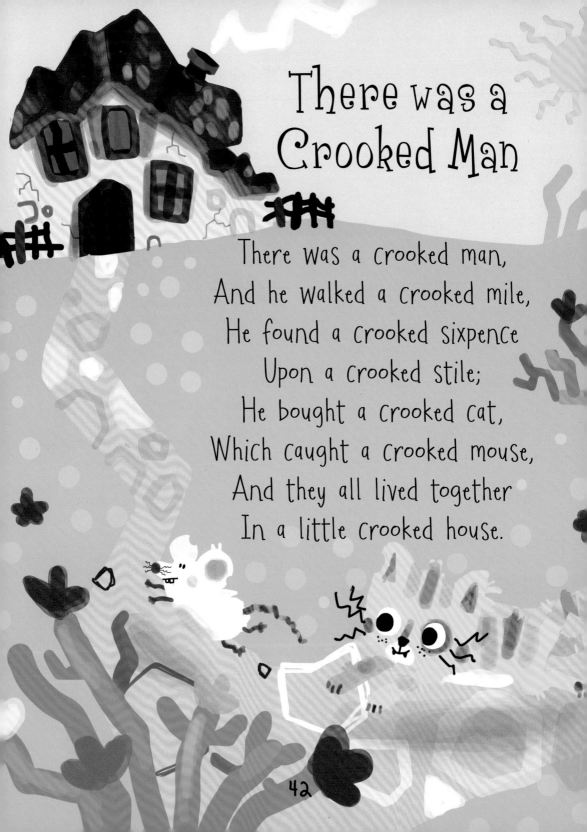

There was a Crooked Man

There was a crooked man,
And he walked a crooked mile,
He found a crooked sixpence
Upon a crooked stile;
He bought a crooked cat,
Which caught a crooked mouse,
And they all lived together
In a little crooked house.

One, Two, Three, Four, Five

One, two, three, four, five,
Once I caught a fish alive.
Six, seven, eight, nine, ten,
Then I let it go again.

Why did you let it go?
Because it bit my finger so.
Which finger did it bite?
This little finger on
my right.

The North Wind Doth Blow

The North wind doth blow
and we shall have snow,
And what will poor robin do then,
Poor thing?

He'll sit in a barn
and keep himself warm
And hide his head under his wing,
Poor thing.

GirLs anD BoyS come OuT to pLaY

Girls and boys come out to play,
The moon does shine as bright as day.
Leave your supper, and leave your sleep,
And come with your playfellows
into the street.

Come with a whoop, come with a call,
Come with a good will or not at all.
Up the ladder and down the wall,
A halfpenny loaf will serve us all.
You find milk, and I'll find flour,
And we'll have a pudding
in half an hour.

47

Ring-a-ring o' Roses

Ring-a-ring o' roses,
A pocket full of posies,
A-tishoo! A-tishoo!
We all fall down.

Mix a Pancake

Mix a pancake,
Stir a pancake,
Pop it in the pan;
Fry the pancake;
Toss the pancake,
Catch it if you can.

Mary's Lamb

Mary had a little lamb,
Its fleece was white as snow,
And everywhere that Mary went
The lamb was sure to go.

It followed her to school one day,
Which was against the rule,
It made the children
laugh and play
To see a lamb at school.

And so the teacher turned it out,
But still it lingered near,
And waited patiently about
Till Mary did appear.

"Why does the lamb love Mary so?"
The eager children cry;
"Why, Mary loves the lamb, you know,"
The teacher did reply.

Jumping Joan

Here I am,
Little jumping Joan;
When nobody's with me
I'm all alone.

52

Jack be Nimble

Jack be nimble,
Jack be quick,
Jack jump over the candlestick.

53

Sleep, Baby, Sleep

Sleep, baby, sleep,
Father guards the sheep,
Mother shakes the
    dreamland tree
And from it fall
Sweet dreams for thee,
Sleep, baby, sleep.

Sleep, baby, sleep,
Our cottage vale is deep,
The little lamb is on the green,
The woolly fleece so soft and clean.
Sleep, baby, sleep.

54

Sleep, baby, sleep,
Down where the
woodbines creep,
Be always like the
lamb so mild,
A kind and sweet
and gentle child.
Sleep, baby, sleep.

Little Bo-peep

Little Bo-peep
has lost her sheep
And doesn't know where
to find them.
Leave them alone and
they'll come home,
Bringing their tails
behind them.

Jack and Jill

Jack and Jill went up the hill
To fetch a pail of water.
Jack fell down and broke his crown
And Jill came tumbling after.

Up Jack got and home did trot
As fast as he could caper.
He went to bed to mend his head
With vinegar and brown paper.

Five Little Ducks

Five little ducks went
swimming one day,
Over the hill and
far away.
Mother duck said,
"Quack, quack,
quack, quack!"
And only four little
ducks came back.

Four little ducks went
swimming one day,
Over the hill and
far away.
Mother duck said,
"Quack, quack,
quack, quack!"
And only three little
ducks came back.

Three little ducks
went swimming
one day,
Over the hill and
far away.
Mother duck said,
"Quack, quack,
quack, quack!"
And only two little
ducks came back.

Two little ducks
went swimming
one day,
Over the hill and
far away.
Mother duck said,
"Quack, quack,
quack, quack!"
And only one little
duck came back.

One little duck went
swimming one day,
Over the hill and far away.
Mother duck said,
"Quack, quack,
        quack, quack!"
And all her five little
ducks came back.

Rub-a-dub-dub

Rub-a-dub-dub,
Three men in a tub,
And who do you think they be?
The butcher, the baker,
The candlestick maker,
And all of them going to sea.

The Lion and the Unicorn

The lion and the unicorn
Were fighting for the crown;
The lion beat the unicorn
All around the town.

Some gave them white bread
And some gave them brown;
Some gave them plum cake
And drummed them
out of town!

63

Bye Baby Bunting

Bye baby bunting,
Daddy's gone a-hunting,
To get a little
rabbit-skin,

To wrap his little baby in.

The Man in the Moon

The man in the moon
Looked out of the moon,
And this is what he said,
"Tis time that now
I'm getting up,
All babies went to bed."

The Grand Old Duke of York

Oh, the grand old Duke of York,
He had ten thousand men,
He marched them up to the top of the hill
And he marched them down again.

And when they were up they were up,
And when they were down they were down,
And when they were only halfway up,

They were neither up nor down.

Six Little Mice

Six little mice sat down to spin,
Pussycat passed and she peeped in.
"What are you doing, my little men?"
"Weaving coats for gentlemen."

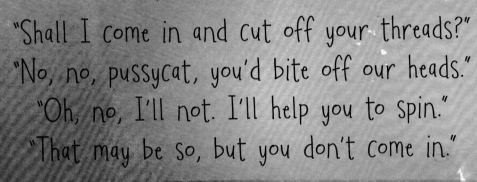

"Shall I come in and cut off your threads?"
"No, no, pussycat, you'd bite off our heads."
"Oh, no, I'll not. I'll help you to spin."
"That may be so, but you don't come in."

Rain, Rain

Rain, rain, go away,
Come again another day.

Rain, rain, go away,
Little Johnny wants to play.

One, Two, Three, Four

One, two, three, four,
Mary at the
kitchen door.
Five, six, seven, eight,
Eating cherries
off a plate.

71

Little Boy Blue

Little Boy Blue,
Come blow your horn,
The sheep's in the meadow,
The cow's in the corn.

But where is the boy
Who looks after the sheep?
He's under a haystack,
Fast asleep!

Will you wake him?
No, not I,
For if I do,
He'll surely cry.

73

Hush, Little Baby

Hush, little baby, don't say a word,
Papa's going to buy you a mockingbird.
If that mockingbird won't sing,
Papa's going to buy you a diamond ring.
If that diamond ring turns to brass,
Papa's going to buy you a looking-glass.

If that looking-glass gets broke,
Papa's going to buy you a billy-goat.
If that billy-goat runs away,
Papa's going to buy you
another today.

One for Sorrow

One for sorrow,
Two for joy,
Three for a girl,
Four for a boy.
Five for silver,

Six for gold,
Seven for a secret,
Never to be told.
Eight for a wish,
Nine for a kiss,

Ten for a bird you want to miss.

Oh Where, Oh Where has my Little Dog Gone?

Oh where, oh where
Has my little dog gone?
Oh where, oh where can he be?

With his ears cut short
And his tail cut long
Oh where, oh where can he be?

79

See-saw, Margery Daw

See-saw, Margery Daw,
Johnny shall have a new master,
He shall have but a penny a day
Because he can't work any faster.

I Hear Thunder

I hear thunder, I hear thunder,
Hark, don't you, hark, don't you?
Pitter patter raindrops,
Pitter patter raindrops,
I'm wet through,
So are you.

Little Jack Horner

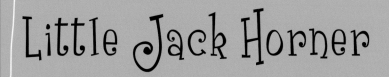

Little Jack Horner
Sat in the corner,
Eating his Christmas pie;
He put in a thumb,
And pulled out a plum,
And said, "What a good boy am I."

If all the World were Paper

If all the world were paper,
And all the sea were ink,
If all the trees were bread and cheese,
What should we have to drink?

Three Little Kittens

Three little kittens, they lost their mittens,
And they began to cry,
"Oh mother dear, we sadly fear,
That we have lost our mittens."
"What! Lost your mittens, you naughty kittens!
Then you shall have no pie.
Meow, meow, meow.
Then you shall have no pie."

The three little kittens, they found their mittens,
And they began to cry,
"Oh mother dear, see here, see here,
For we have found our mittens."
"Put on your mittens, you silly kittens,
And you shall have some pie."
"Purr, purr, purr,
Oh, let us have some pie."

The three little kittens
put on their mittens,
And soon ate up the pie.
"Oh mother dear, we greatly fear,
That we have soiled our mittens."
"What, soiled your mittens,
you naughty kittens!"
Then they began to sigh,
"Meow, meow, meow,"
Then they began to sigh.

The three little kittens,
they washed their mittens,
And hung them out to dry.
"Oh mother dear, do you not hear,
That we have washed our mittens?"
"What, washed your mittens,
then you're good kittens,
But I smell a rat close by."
"Meow, meow, meow,
We smell a rat close by."

87

Rain

Rain on the green grass,
Rain on the trees,
Rain on the rooftop,
But not on me!

88

It's Raining

It's raining, it's pouring,
The old man is snoring;
He went to bed

And bumped his head
And couldn't get up in the morning!

Diddle Diddle Dumpling

Diddle diddle dumpling,
My son John,
Went to bed
With his trousers on.
One shoe off,
And one shoe on,
Diddle diddle dumpling,
My son John.

I had a Little Nut Tree

I had a little nut tree,
Nothing would it bear
But a silver nutmeg
And a golden pear;

The King of Spain's daughter
Came to visit me,
And all for the sake
Of my little nut tree.

93

Mary, Mary

Mary, Mary, quite contrary,
How does your garden grow?
With silver bells and cockle shells,
And pretty maids all in a row.

Baa, Baa, Black Sheep

Baa, baa, black sheep,
Have you any wool?
Yes, sir, yes, sir,
Three bags full.
One for the master,
One for the dame,
And one for the little boy
Who lives down the lane.

I Saw Three Ships

I saw three ships come sailing by,
Come sailing by, come sailing by,
I saw three ships come sailing by,
On New Year's Day in the morning.

And what do you think was in them then,
Was in them then, was in them then?
And what do you think was in them then,
On New Year's Day in the morning?

Three pretty girls were in them then,
Were in them then, were in them then,
Three pretty girls were in them then,
On New Year's Day in the morning.

This Little Pig

Market

This little pig went to market,
This little pig stayed at home,
This little pig had roast beef,
This little pig had none,
And this little pig cried,
"Wee-Wee-
    wee-Wee-Wee!"
All the way home.

99

Old Mother Hubbard

Old Mother Hubbard
Went to the cupboard
To get her poor dog
a bone.

100

But when she got there
The cupboard was bare,
And so, the poor dog had none.

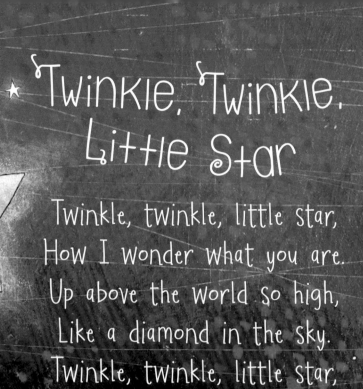

Twinkle, Twinkle, Little Star

Twinkle, twinkle, little star,
How I wonder what you are.
Up above the world so high,
Like a diamond in the sky.
Twinkle, twinkle, little star,
How I wonder what you are.

Star Light, Star Bright

Star light, star bright,
First star I see tonight.
I wish I may, I wish I might,
Have the wish I wish tonight.

Hot Cross Buns!

Hot cross buns! Hot cross buns!
One a penny, two a penny,
Hot cross buns!
Give them to your daughters,
Give them to your sons,
One a penny, two a penny,
Hot cross buns!

Hickety Pickety

Hickety pickety my black hen,
She lays eggs for gentlemen.
Sometimes nine and
sometimes ten,
Hickety pickety my black hen.

Father's Day

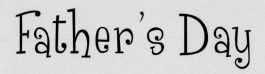

"Walk a little slower, Daddy,"
said a child so small.
"I'm following in your footsteps
and I don't want to fall.

Sometimes your steps are very fast,
Sometimes they're hard to see;
So, walk a little slower, Daddy,
For you are leading me.

Someday when I'm all grown up,
You're what I want to be;
Then I will have a little child
Who'll want to follow me.

And I would want to lead just right,
And know that I was true;
So walk a little slower, Daddy,
For I must follow you."

Little Tommy Tucker

Little Tommy Tucker
Sings for his supper.

What shall we give him?
White bread and butter.

How shall he cut it
Without a knife?

How will he be married
Without a wife?

109

Pussycat Mole

Pussycat Mole
Jumped over a coal,
And in her best petticoat
Burnt a great hole.

Poor pussycat's weeping
She'll have no more milk
Until her best petticoat's
Mended with silk.

Ladybird, Ladybird

Ladybird, ladybird fly away home,
Your house is on fire and
your children are gone,
All except one, and her name is Ann,
And she hid under the frying pan.

Teddy Bear, Teddy Bear

Teddy bear, teddy bear, touch the ground.
Teddy bear, teddy bear, turn around.
Teddy bear, teddy bear, show your shoe.
Teddy bear, teddy bear, that will do.

Teddy bear, teddy bear, run upstairs.
Teddy bear, teddy bear, say your prayers.
Teddy bear, teddy bear, blow out the light.
Teddy bear, teddy bear,
Say GOODNIGHT.

POLLY PUT THE KETTLE ON

Polly put the
kettle on,
Polly put the
kettle on,
Polly put the
kettle on,
And let's have tea.

Sukey take it off again,
Sukey take it off again,
Sukey take it off again,
They've all gone away.

Two Little Dicky Birds

Two little dicky birds sitting on a wall,
One named Peter, one named Paul.
Fly away Peter, fly away Paul,
Come back Peter, come back Paul!

Whether the Weather

Whether the weather be fine,
Or whether the weather be not,
Whether the weather be cold,
Or whether the weather be hot,

We'll weather the weather
Whatever the weather,
Whether we like it or not!

Two Cats of Kilkenny

There once were two cats of Kilkenny,
Each thought there was one cat too many,
So they fought and they fit,
And they scratched and they bit,

Till, excepting their nails
And the tips of their tails,

Instead of two cats,
there weren't any.

118

Peter Piper

Peter Piper picked
a peck of pickled peppers;

A peck of pickled peppers
Peter Piper picked.

If Peter Piper picked
a peck of pickled peppers,

Where's the peck
of pickled peppers
Peter Piper picked?

120

121

The Mulberry Bush

Here we go round the mulberry bush,
The mulberry bush, the mulberry bush,
Here we go round the mulberry bush,
On a cold and frosty morning.

Hey Diddle Diddle

Hey diddle diddle,
The cat and the fiddle,
The cow jumped over the moon;
The little dog laughed
To see such fun,
And the dish ran away with the spoon.

Itsy Bitsy
Spider

Itsy Bitsy Spider
Climbed up the water spout,
Down came the rain
And washed the spider out.

124

Out came the sun
And dried up all the rain,
So Itsy Bitsy Spider
Climbed up the spout again!

The Muffin Man

Do you know the muffin man,
The muffin man, the muffin man,
Do you know the muffin man,
Who lives in Drury Lane?

Yes, I know the muffin man,
The muffin man, the muffin man,
Yes, I know the muffin man,
Who lives in Drury Lane.

Pussycat, Pussycat

Pussycat, pussycat, where have you been?
I've been up to London to visit the queen!

Pussycat, pussycat, what did you there?
I frightened a little mouse under the chair!

Rock-a-bye Baby

Rock-a-bye baby,

On the treetop.
When the wind blows
The cradle will rock.

When the bough breaks

The cradle will fall.
Down will come baby,
Cradle and all.

The Wheels on the Bus

The wheels on the bus go
round and round,
Round and round,
round and round.
The wheels on
the bus go
round and round,
All day long.

132

The horn on the bus goes
Beep, beep, beep,
Beep, beep, beep,
Beep, beep, beep.
The horn on
the bus goes
Beep, beep, beep,
All day long.

The windshield
wipers go
Swish, swish, swish,
Swish, swish, swish,
Swish, swish, swish,
The windshield
wipers go
Swish, swish, swish,
All day long.

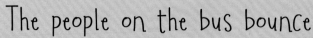

The people on the bus bounce
up and down,
Up and down,
up and down.
The people on
the bus bounce
up and down,
All day long.

How many Miles to Babylon?

How many miles to Babylon?
Three score miles and ten.
Can I get there by candlelight?
Aye, and back again.
If your feet are nimble and light,
You may get there by
candlelight.

Little Girl, Little Girl

Little girl, little girl,
Where have you been?
Gathering roses
To give to the queen.

Little girl, little girl,
What gave she you?
She gave me a diamond
As big as my shoe.

136

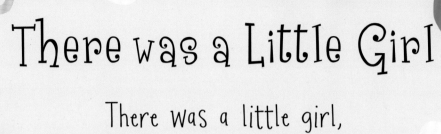

There was a Little Girl

There was a little girl,
and she had a little curl,
Right in the middle of her forehead;
When she was good,
she was very, very good,
But when she was bad, she was horrid!

If all the Seas were One Sea

If all the seas were one sea,
What a great sea that would be!
If all the trees were one tree,
What a great tree that would be!

If all the axes were one axe,
What a great axe that would be!
If all the men were one man,
What a great man that would be!

And if the great man took the great axe
And cut down the great tree,
And let it fall into the great sea,
What a great splish-splash that would be!

To Market, to Market

To market, to market
to buy a fat pig;
Home again, home again,
jiggety-jig.

To market, to market
to buy a fat hog;
Home again, home again,
jiggety-jog.

One Potato

One potato, two potato,
Three potato, four;
Five potato, six potato,
Seven potato more.

Round and Round the Garden

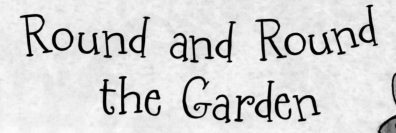

Round and round
the garden
Like a teddy bear.
One step, two step,
Tickle you under there!

As I was Going to St Ives

St Ives

As I was going to St Ives,
I met a man with seven wives,
Each wife had seven sacks,
Each sack had seven cats,
Each cat had seven kits:
Kits, cats, sacks, and wives,
How many were there
going to St Ives?

Here is the Church

Here is the church, and here is the steeple,
Open the door and here are the people.
Here is the parson going upstairs,
And here he is a-saying his prayers.

Pease porridge Hot

Pease porridge hot,
Pease porridge cold,
Pease porridge in the pot
Nine days old.

Some like it hot,
Some like it cold,
Some like it in the pot
Nine days old!

Lavender's Blue

Lavender's blue, dilly, dilly,
Lavender's green,
When I am King, dilly, dilly,
You shall be Queen.

Who told you so, dilly, dilly,
Who told you so?
'Twas my own heart, dilly, dilly,
That told me so.

Call up your men, dilly, dilly,
Set them to work,
Some to the plough, dilly, dilly,
Some to the cart.

Some to make hay, dilly, dilly,
Some to make corn,
While you and I, dilly, dilly,
Keep ourselves warm.

Lavender's green, dilly, dilly,
Lavender's blue,
If you love me, dilly, dilly,
I will love you.

Blow, Wind, Blow

Blow, wind, blow,
And go, mill, go;
That the miller
May grind his corn;
That the baker may take it,
And into bread make it,
And bring us some
Hot in the morn.

Five Little Pussycats

Five little pussycats playing
near the door,
One ran and hid inside
And then there were four.

Four little pussycats
underneath a tree,
One heard a dog bark
And then there were three.

Three little pussycats
thinking what to do,
One saw a little bird
And then there were two.

153

Two little pussycats
sitting in the sun,
One ran to catch his tail
And then there was one.

One little pussycat looking
for some fun,
He saw a butterfly
And then there were none.

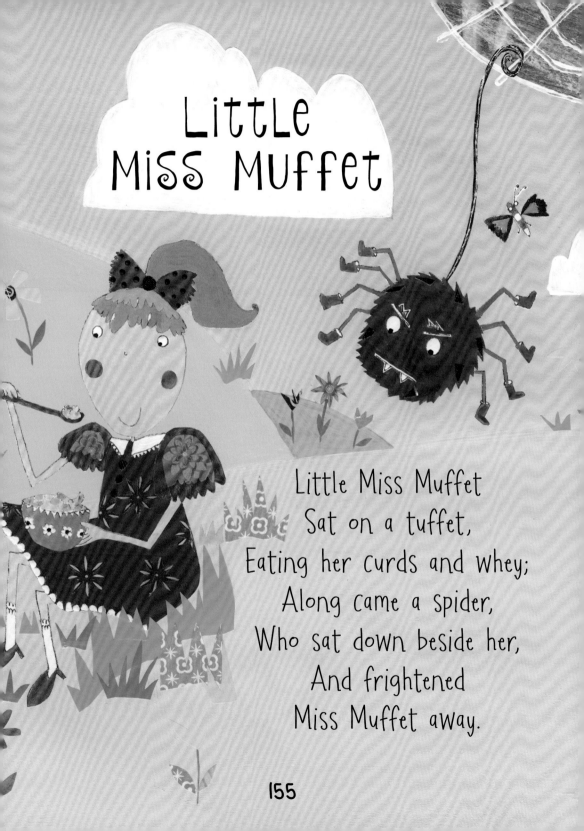

Little Miss Muffet

Little Miss Muffet
Sat on a tuffet,
Eating her curds and whey;
Along came a spider,
Who sat down beside her,
And frightened
Miss Muffet away.

Row, Row, Row your Boat

Row, row, row your boat
Gently down the stream.
Merrily, merrily, merrily, merrily,
Life is but a dream.

Jack Sprat

Jack Sprat could eat no fat,
His wife could eat no lean,
So between them both, you see,
They licked the platter clean.

Jack ate all the lean,
Joan ate all the fat,
The bone they picked it clean,
Then gave it to the cat.

There was an Old Woman

There was an old woman
Tossed up in a basket,
Seventeen times as high as the moon.
Where she was going
I just had to ask it,
For in her hand she carried a broom.

"Old woman, old woman, old woman," said I,
"O whither, O whither, O whither so high?"
"I'm sweeping the cobwebs
Down from the sky!
And I'll be with you
By and by."

The Evening is Coming

The evening is coming,
The sun sinks to rest,
The birds are all flying
Straight home to the nest.

"Caw," says the crow
As he flies overhead,
"It's time little children
Were going to bed!"